The Minimalist Budget

A Practical Guide On How To Save Money, Spend Less And Live More With A Minimalist Lifestyle

A guide to the gypsy life

Table Of Contents

Introduction: What is Minimalist Budgeting?

What's the first thing you think of when you hear the word "budget"? It's a meager little word, one that all too often comes after "tight". Maybe you think of this word as an adjective, something to describe a cheap and substandard car or hotel. "Budget" brings to mind rationing, a kind of money diet. If you're like many people, budgeting is something you do with a kind of deflated spirit: budgeting means bargain bin quality and the sad sense that what you want is going to be just out of reach.

This book will try a different approach to budgeting all together. It's a pity that the idea of living within one's means should be experienced as such a deficit – this book will try to show that when you apply the principles of minimalism to budgeting, you are neither in a state of self-denial or trying to survive a financial scrape. In fact, a minimalist budget is a particular approach to abundance and fulfillment that may seem counterintuitive to most.

Undoubtedly, what came into your mind when you heard the word "budget" was simple: money. Money is a thing to be feared, to be saved, to be celebrated when it's there and mourned when it isn't. Budgeting, we are told, is necessary.

When you live in a world where there is always one more thing to buy, being cognizant of the fact that you don't have endless resources is just the practical thing to do.

However, budgeting can be much more than this. To put it simply, money is only *one* of the resources that we should be managing in our lives, and possibly not even the most important one.

As humans, it is our lot to deal with being finite beings: we have only so much time to spend on this earth, only so much time that we are allotted each day, only so much energy that we can give away before we run into a deficit.

In a sense, the principles of minimalism rest on a more fundamental interpretation of "budget". Just as you need to match your financial expenditure with your income, minimalism encourages us to match our needs with our actions. It doesn't make sense to buy food for 12 when you have a family of 4 in the same way it doesn't make sense to clutter up your home with things you don't want, like or need. Trimming away at unessential elements in your day-to-day life is an exercise in budgeting and minimalism both, whether you are trimming away excess expenses, destructive thoughts or junk in your spare room.

This book will offer an expanded notion of what it means to budget. We'll look at how money is not the only resource that needs to be managed, and a "life budget" that acknowledges your emotional, behavioral, social and even spiritual capital is more likely to lead to smarter decisions.

Minimalism is not, of course, about starvation or punishment. It's not about doing with less than you need. Rather, minimalism is about finding what you need and fulfilling that need exactly, without excess. It's a subtle point and one that the average person who has grown up in an industrialized capitalist society can miss: *to have exactly enough is not suffering.* Budgeting is therefore about understanding what you need to have enough, and how best you can allocate your resources to that end.

Most of the budgeting advice out there will come firmly out of the scarcity paradigm – you're usually offered a few ways to shave off money here and there. You are asked to look at all the instances where you are not spending or living on the bare minimum, and usually anything extra is framed as unnecessary, indulgent or, depending on who you talk to, bordering on immoral. These tips will tell you that after enough cheap toothpaste, homemade laundry soap and clothes bought out of season, you'll save enough money and make it all work. You're asked to look over your life and find places where you could manage, without too much discomfort, to do with less or even without.

While thriftiness and being money-conscious are excellent skills to have (and for some, absolutely necessary), minimalist budgeting is more about conscious decision making and less about stinginess and trying to endure a lack.

To show the difference, consider a purchase someone might make: a new dishwasher. On paper, the initial cost of a dishwasher might make it look like a kind of luxury. After all, you can simply wash the dishes *for free* yourself, right? In traditional budgetland, a dishwasher may fall well into the category of "unnecessary". Can you do without it? Of course. Then, it doesn't belong in your pared down budget. On the face of it, this logic seems sound. In fact, while you're laboring away washing dishes by hand, you may even get the impression that doing it all yourself is kind of noble.

The "minimalist budgeting" in this book will ask you to take a more expanded view of the dishwasher. Not buying one will certainly result in less of your money spent. But, as mentioned, since money is not your only resource, by focusing on only this aspect you're not getting the full picture. Is the cost of doing dishes by hand *really* free? In your budget, have you factored in the fact that washing dishes saps hours of your life each week and makes you grumpy? If you're so wiped out at the prospect of another 45 minutes of housework at the end of the day that you give up and splash out on expensive restaurant food, you haven't even saved money, anyway.

When you lay alone in bed at night and ponder your existence, which will mean more to you: the extra cash you saved by not buying a dishwasher, or the lifestyle you gave up as the person who never has to worry about dishes again? You can't take your possessions with you when you die, they say, but which will be more soothing to you on your deathbed - the fact that your life was thrifty or that it was enjoyable and meaningful?

Simple budgeting doesn't take these kinds of things into account. The primary purpose of your life, at least in some sense, is to be happy. Money usually facilitates this. But if you're maximizing your money to the point that it makes you less happy, your budget is no longer serving its purpose. Minimalist budgeting is like regular budgeting, only with an eye to what is truly important. While this book will certainly show you nifty ways to save a buck here and there, it will also regularly ask you to examine what that buck means to you at the end of the day.

We'll explore shopping and spending habits, identify problem areas, think about debt and make achievable goals for home, work and more. We'll look at concrete ways to put some of these principles into action, and look at resources that will keep you focused and motivated. But at the same time, this book is also about the philosophy of minimalism, not thriftiness. If you can pair your budget plan with a more nuanced understanding of your relationship with money and how it ties into how you want to live, the changes you make will be more authentic and longer lasting.

Chapter 1: The Purchase

Let's start at the very beginning – the moment when we buy something, when money changes hands and we go home with a new item that suddenly is part of our lives. The fact that so many people buy things when they barely even thought of buying them before they actually stepped into a shop speaks to the power of advertising. The typical shopping experience is an exercise in mindlessness. In fact, one of its primary characteristics is that you can't think about it for too long – otherwise you'd probably come to your senses and leave with the same amount of money you came in with. If you've ever arrived at home and looked at a purchase, almost as if for the first time, and regretted it deeply, you've fallen victim to the forces that can trap the mindless customer.

Mindful consuming means having principles set firmly in place before going into this fray. When you know what you want and why, you're somewhat immune to advertising. If you waltz into a shop without a firm sense of why you're there and what you need and want, you're basically inviting the forces of marketing to come and take your money and time from you. Here are some ways to become a more savvy consumer:

Avoid going to shops and malls when you feel tired, sad or bored

Advertising doesn't appeal to your highest self; it speaks to your weakness – your emotions of greed or fear. For advertising of most items to work, the customer needs to feel that they are lacking somehow: your children's clothes are filthy, your phone is old and outdated, you look and feel terrible and only a new X can fix the problem. If you enter into a retail space already in a compromised mood, you'll be even more primed to receive these messages. For much of the Western world, people are encouraged to solve problems by buying things. Be mindful of negative emotions and be careful of making decisions when you are trying to escape them.

Get a real sense of your options

As modern day hunter-gatherers, we have a long history of ferreting out a good bargain, or finding exactly the item that we need. It's no exaggeration that the quality of our choices can never be better than the quality of the options we have at hand. If you are simply not aware of something better, you can't possibly choose it. Don't be a person who makes poor purchasing choices simply because you didn't know any better. There may be a close and convenient store that you always go to, but ask yourself, are there any other options worth considering? Could you buy your item online? A common advertising trick is to provide the customer with plenty of options – but don't forget: you can always *not* choose and go somewhere else where the choices are different.

Have a plan

Spur-of-the-moment style decisions can work out OK sometimes, but more often than not, choices made spontaneously only serve to increase confusion and dim focus in your life. Before you head out to shop, visualize what you need and why. Imagine a filter going down over your eyes that allows you to only perceive what is relevant. Write a list if it helps, and plan to go when you have adequate time and the shops will not be too busy.

Be realistic

People build entire careers out of making merchandise look more appealing to you in the store. Lighting, special displays and music make everything look better. You may unconsciously buy into the hype that a mannequin and special marketing help to create around a particular item of clothing, for instance. You then get home and realize: you simply bought a very ordinary sweater. Try, as much as you can, to take each item and imagine it in your actual life. How will this fit you? Will your family *actually* eat this? Where in your day do you plan to use this new gadget?

Learn to look for quality

Get into the habit of examining the workmanship of new items. Check seams of clothing, look at how tools or toys are constructed, examine the warranties of appliances and think of how much maintenance each item will require once purchased. Never buy an item with the intention of it only lasting a short time. Just the same as you imagine a new item and how it will fit with your life, try to imagine what it will look in a year or two.

Keep it simple

Food, for example, is an area where there is a lot of "added value" thrown into the mix. You wrote "potatoes" on your list but now you see that there are at least five different options for potatoes – different prices, different degrees of being pre-processed, organic or nonorganic etc. If you only wrote "potatoes", there's a strong chance this item in your life is simply not that important to stress about. Don't waste another 5 minutes of your existence trying to maximize on a decision that, truthfully, means very little to you. Buy any old potatoes and get on with it. This frees up time to track down and optimize the more specific needs you have, for example the other possible item on your list, "Two bottles of fresh orange juice – the one with the green label."

Keep your other resources in mind

You've probably heard the advice that buying fresh vegetables is cheaper than ones that are pre-cut or processed somehow. This is true. But with an eye to minimalism and not just thriftiness (or worse, being cheap), we need to consider the bigger picture. A bag of bulk, unwashed and unpeeled potatoes may save you a little money. But before you reach for them, add into the price your time and effort it will take to cut and peel them yourself. If you can earn more money in your job during the time it would take you to cut and peel than the money you save by buying the cheaper version, then you haven't really saved anything. In fact, you've lost money and purposefully chosen to fill your time – your other precious resource – with potato peeling. Sometimes time really is money – strike a balance.

Think in relative terms

Get into the habit of looking at the price of things in terms of the price of other things. $100 may not seem like much for such a fabulous new gadget, but when you think of it in terms of costing the same as 20 cups of coffee, two shirts or food for your dog for a month, you get a little more perspective. Better yet, frame it in terms of hours you'd need to work. Is the item worth, say, four hours of your life? Let's be dramatic here, it's not four hours of work you're paying, it's four hours of time, also known as... your life.

Commit to not comparing yourself to others

Thank goodness for advertisers that human beings are such insecure social creatures. How much has been bought in the history of the world simply to keep up with someone else who bought something too? How much of the value of an item is merely the value of everyone else's approval? Don't pressure yourself into buying something just because you feel like it's the thing people should do. We like to think we grow out of this peer pressure with age, but many an adult has taken on ungodly amounts of debt to buy their homes simply because that's what the world expects of people their particular age.

If all else fails, don't give money to people who tell you that you suck

90% of advertising is based on telling you how awful and stupid your life is without their product. Do you want to reward this kind of thing by giving these people your money?

Chapter 2: Making Your Budget, Part One: Finding the Core

Because this book is not just about financial budgeting, but takes into account other important factors, too, our budgets are going to be a little different. Our main goal for this expanded type of budget is to find that sweet spot in between what we want and need, and the resources we have to give towards this end – not just money.

Perhaps you're familiar with Oscar Wilde's advice: when you only have two pennies left in the world, spend one on bread and the other on a lily. Oscar may have been a bit flamboyant, but he understood something about budgeting and value. He valued his own inspiration, his own sense of well being and believing that the world was a beautiful place *as much as* he valued the need to eat. For Oscar, being filled up with twice as much bread was simply not worth it if you had neglected to nourish your soul. That we want to be mindful and smart with our money is a given. But there are two other resources that people routinely forget to factor into their budgets: time and value.

Time

Your salary could always change, and even if you lose your job, you'll likely have some savings or a severance package to tide you over for a while. It's always possible to borrow or lend money, or, in that case, steal it even. Time is not so forgiving. All we know is that we are alive right now – how much time we still have is anyone's guess, and we could suddenly run out in an instant. Money can be made and spent, but time is more fixed. We will all die. None of us, no matter our station in life, wakes up to the luxury of more than 24 hours each day. In this, we are all equal.

Trading in time for money is the basis of all work – you sell a piece of your work and effort (i.e. your time) in exchange for money. This works out fine if you intend to use that money to enrich the remaining time you have, but sadly, people can forget this part of the dynamic. The balance between time and money is forgotten about – we make choices as if time was infinite and money was the most important.

Rather than begin with money, a solid minimalist budget begins with time, the most absolute and precious of your resources. You may feel it's counterproductive to dawdle with your time management when your credit card debt needs attention, but the two are inextricably linked. A budget that takes into account money will only ever solve half of your problems.

Begin with the capital you have: 24 hours each day, seven days in each week. Decide on your needs and work backwards. Sleep is a good place to start – you may block out seven or eight hours of each day to sleep. Next block out time taken for meals, exercise and grooming. Try not to be idealistic – you may think you only spend an hour each morning getting ready, but be honest and look at what you really spend. No time is "dead". If you feel like you need at least an hour to unwind and do nothing at the end of each day, factor that in.

When you begin to break down your life in this way, you may notice how much of your time is frittered away on things that you don't ultimately care about. People lament the lack of quality relaxation time they have in their lives and yet waste hours on TV or trashy websites that add nothing to their experience. This points to a problem in time budgeting: sometimes, our spending habits are not in tune with our values and goals.

Just as you don't want to pay extra for an insurance service you have no need for, you don't want to use up your time in a way that doesn't fit your main goals. At the end of the day, no matter what you have done, the 24 hours is up, and your decisions are made. End of story. The fact that our lives are finite is scary enough – to know that you squandered what you had on looking at gossip on the Internet or flipping past infomercials on the couch will make this fact even harder to swallow.

The thing about time is that it's not possible to go into debt – if you spend more time on a task than you really want to, that time is taken away from something else. Zoning out in front of a game seems pretty innocuous, until you think that that activity is actively *displacing* another one. In other words, it's an opportunity cost, and you're usually losing out on other, better opportunities.

When you choose to play computer games for 4 hours straight you are making a choice, even if you don't think you are: you are saying that this activity is more important than anything else you could be doing at the moment. Better than spending time with those you love, better than learning to play that instrument you've been meaning to, better than exercise or a good meal or sex. So, is it? Budgeting your time is asking yourself this deliberately: is this the best way to spend your time?

Here's a clue that you have been squandering your time: you're always busy but feel like you never have any time. You go to bed at night with the creeping suspicion that, on the grand "to do" list of life, you've forgotten to tick something off. You get depressed on Sunday evenings thinking about going back to work. You feel old. You say to people around you, "Hey, where did September go?"

Value

The second valuable resource is a little more subtle. For the most part, money is a stand-in for "value". It is a symbol of worth that we attach to things, and entire economies are built on the patterns that emerge when we all agree on how much an item is worth. Usually, money is a pretty accurate indicator of something's value. But the important thing is that an item's monetary value is not fixed, and certainly not absolute. An item's value shifts with something more fundamental: our *perception* of its value.

An example: someone may sell you a gadget that is worth exactly $10. In a real and indisputable way, this item is "worth" $10. Yet, whether this item translates to $10 of *value* in your life, in your actual lived experience, is something completely different. Your quality of life, your well-being and your sense of achieving your own *personal* goals may or may not coincide with the market value of $10 given to this item. On the ground, such an item may provide you the equivalent of $20 in peace of mind and happiness, or drain you of $10 in the form of extra stress and fuss.

The only one that can decide an item's real-life value is you –
the person living the life. Money is a stand in only – we need
to learn to consistently ask ourselves what value things bring
to our lives, regardless of what the market tells us they are
worth.

Budgeting with an eye to more fundamental value means
asking what things add to the experience of your being alive.
The tone of your living, the texture of how you move about,
interact with people, how you feel about yourself, your well-
being and sense of purpose, these are all hidden yet extremely
important parts of your decision-making process. You may
end up going with the unwashed and unpeeled potatoes in the
end because you realize that the experience of spending time
in your kitchen is quality time and something you cherish.

You cannot add more time to your day or your life, but you *can*
enhance the quality of the time that you do have. Time passed
well is the experience of value. Passing time in a way that feels
satisfactory is something to seriously consider when you make
choices. Importantly, nobody can tell you what you value. If
you read a book encouraging you to spend more special time
with your children, you may never realize the simple fact that
you are quite happy with how much time you spend with them
already. Then you may wonder why spending more quality

time with them only seems to aggravate everyone involved. The choice you made that was intended to make you happier is actually doing precisely the opposite.

The simple way to find out how to factor value into your budget is to become aware of what really matters to you. What is the point of your life? When do you feel most energized, happiest and most fulfilled? If you don't build into your life moments where you actively pursue these principles, then you cannot be surprised when you get to the end of it and feel as though it's all been a waste. It's sad that many people feel like their true passions and values are more of an afterthought, something to indulge in only after they fulfill all their obligations. The problem with this approach is that once you fulfill those obligations, you'll probably be left with a sense of emptiness: what was it all for anyway?

A budget will be more effective and more meaningful if it takes into account the fact that you are a human being who has a real need to be emotionally and spiritually fulfilled. If practically that means you are unwilling to devote anything less than three hours a week to choir practice, then blocking that in becomes as fixed and permanent as the need for sleep.

Chapter 3: Making Your Budget, Part Two: Cutting

Now that you've identified the parts of your life that are non-negotiable, you can turn your attention to the parts that are less so. By drawing a line around the things that are unchangeable (the amount of time you have) and the things that you don't *want* to change (your passions and values) you are left with the parts of your life that can be practically moderated. Vow to not touch these important aspects. If you have allotted yourself an hour each day to pursuing something that is deeply important to you, don't shortchange yourself by sacrificing that hour to admin or errands when in a pinch. It may not feel like it matters much now, but believe that the loss of well being and sense of purpose in the present becomes important, sooner or later.

This section will most strongly resemble the traditional budgeting advice you may have encountered so far. The principle is simple: if it's not that important, it won't be a big deal to reduce the amount of resources you allocate to it. A dysfunctional budget doesn't reflect your true values. For example, if what you crave more than anything is alone time and the bliss of zoning out with a mindless book, your budget is dysfunctional if there is no time that acknowledges that. More obviously, if you don't care much about what coffee you drink in the morning and simply care about getting caffeine in your system in the quickest way possible, it doesn't make sense to splash out on expensive cappuccinos every day. If your mother drilled it into you since you were little that superhero figurines were a sad and embarrassing way to spend your time and money, a good budget for you may be realizing that, actually, to hell with it, those figurines make you really, really happy.

Again, the difference between regular budgeting and minimalist budgeting: we are not attempting to remove everything, but to remove that which doesn't serve us or is unnecessary to our deep sense of value. The paradox is that trimming away the clutter often allows us to enjoy our true passions *more*, not less. Freed of distraction and the need to maintain pointless rubbish in our day-to-day life, we can turn our full attention to the things we are happy to dedicate hours and money to.

Using the tips provided later in this book as inspiration, make a thorough inventory of every single point of expenditure during a month period. It may help you to convert these figures into percentages (percentage of total expenditure), which give a better *relative* value of how they compare to other expenses. For example, you may find that you spend $70 on average every month on your superhero figurine habit.

But when you look at the rest of the list, other than spending time with your baby nephew, this ranks as the most enjoyable activity in your life. In the next column, allocate a *value* percentage – this is the beginning stage of setting budget goals for yourself. How much does this item add to your life? How much, percentage wise, are you willing to devote of your total income to this hobby? If it were the one thing that makes you really happy, then it'd be fair to say you can allocate a full 10% of your income to this. Why not? People struggle their whole lives to find happiness - if you've found it, then nourish it. So if your salary is $2000, and you only spend $70 of it on figurines when in your heart you are willing to spend up to $200, your budget is not right. If anything, your budget has taken into consideration your mother's goals and ideals and not yours.

This ideal percentage also relates back to the concept of time outlined earlier. If you are spending 2% of your total expenditure on magazines, is that an accurate reflection of how much value magazines add to your life? Also, if magazines, on further examination, actually add very little to your life, your ideal percentage will be much, much lower. Perhaps you will realize that they add nothing to your life at all. Think of the time that this magazine adds and takes to your life, and put this in the "time" column. Magazines are the sort of thing that might take an extra half hour a week to flip through, and they need to be bought and then thrown away. Tally this up and put it in the time column. How many hours do you lose to this activity you feel so-so about? A dishwasher, for example, would have a positive value, since it allows you to save the time you would have spent washing dishes by hand.

Go through each group of items. You needn't be too exact, only keep to the spirit of tallying up each item's true impact and cost on your life. It may emerge that your budget is spent on things that you don't care about or which actively make your life worse. Do you notice how little time and money you spend on your own values? It may turn out that you only *think* you are spending a certain amount of time, money and energy on something but are spending much more or less. This exercise can show you the discrepancies that may exist between your ideal lifestyle and the one you actually live.

"Cutting" a budget sounds bad, doesn't it? But as you turn your attention to what needs to be sliced away, think of it as spring cleaning. A minimalist budget isn't just about reduction and frugality, it's about *efficiency*. As you chop away at your monthly expenditure, think of it as making way for the things that really matter to you. First look at money that is spent on things you don't value. Cut it away. Look at things that take more time than is strictly justified. A certain item may be fine when looked at in financial terms, but when you consider the time drain, would be better eliminated or reduced. Cut it away.

Chapter 4: How to Make "Smart" Goals

If you've spent any time at all living the way you live, you may be rather entrenched in the habit and need some time to "cut" away at certain items. Certain items, people or rituals take time to phase out. This may be as big a deal as moving house or something as trivial as cutting out morning coffee or finding a different route to work.

A "smart" goal is a goal that has the best chance of being achieved. Don't sabotage a good idea by making vague or unreachable goals, like "I'm going to eat better" or "I'm going to stop wasting money on magazines".

A SMART goal is:

Specific

Don't be vague. What does "eat better" mean? More vegetables? How much more? A specific goal is "I'm going to eat vegetables every night with dinner".

Measurable

Simply, how will you know you've achieved your goal? "Buy fewer magazines each month" is not measurable, but "Buy only one magazine each month" is one you can measure.

Attainable

Naturally, only a goal that you can actually achieve is going to be, well, achieved. Be realistic. Making a goal to slash your monthly medication bill when you're managing several chronic illnesses is asking for failure.

Realistic

Related to attainability. We make goals because we aspire to be better, but don't set the bar *too* high. Making the goal to cut your monthly expenditure by half is basically building failure into it.

Time Based

A good goal has an expiration date. "Someday" is giving your unconscious mind permission to slack. Set a date in the future where you expect to reach your goal.

Examples:

Not so smart goal: "I'm going to be more efficient when I do the grocery shopping."

Smart goal: "By this time next month, I'm going to be spending 10% less on groceries."

Not so smart goal: "I'm going to wash my clothes less to save on detergent."

Smart goal: "Tomorrow, I'm going to buy detergent in bulk to save on laundry costs."

Not so smart goal: "I'm going to spend quality time with my children."

Smart goal: "Every Tuesday, I'm going to spend at least one hour with the children playing football."

Chapter 5: The Nitty Gritty

Hopefully, by becoming more aware of what's truly important to you, as well as acknowledging your hard limits (time, money), you're closer to creating a budget that not only saves you money, but offers you the best path to wellness and fulfillment in your life in general, given the fact that our time on this earth is limited.

Once you have identified your values, the time you have available and the money you have coming in, you are better able to cut away at what is unessential to reveal what truly is. This next section will focus more concretely on practical ways you can reduce the time, money and energy you lose to things that ultimately don't serve your highest goals. Since everyone has different sets of resources at their disposal, their solutions are going to be different, too. Some of these solutions won't apply to you, and that's OK. If spending money or time in one area is vital to feeling fulfilled and happy, then you don't need to save money in those areas.

Food

One of the easiest ways to lose track of spending and consequently, one of the easiest places to save money without even trying. Decide on your main motivation and move from there:

When you don't have time to spend on food

If you prioritize convenience over health (naughty!) then it makes sense to splash out on convenience foods. There is no shame in this. Perhaps at this point in your life, you are focused on building your business or are sorting out some other area. Convert your time fussing over food preparation into money which you spend on food delivery services or pre-made meals. The advice to prepare more of your own meals at home is only going to make you more miserable, so chalk up restaurant bills to time saving.

When you don't have money to spend on food

If you prioritize healthy eating, there are plenty of ways to eat healthily without spending too much. If time spent in the kitchen is not an issue, save money by preparing fresh and unprocessed foods yourself. Buy in bulk, cook and freeze. Opt for cheap foods like potatoes, eggs, leafy greens, carrots, pulses and legumes of all kinds and cheap vegetables like cabbage. The money saving tips below are for you.

When you don't have time OR money to spend on food

However, if you want to reduce both time spent on food as well as money, your only choice is to eat foods that are cheap but also require very little preparation. Buy a cookbook that shows you how to prepare food quickly and with only a few ingredients, use a crock-pot and learn to eat mostly salads and simple dishes. Smoothies, three-ingredient meals and sandwiches are your best bet.

Action Steps for shaving money off your food expenditure:

- Make a grocery list and stick to it.

- Don't be embarrassed about buying own-brand food at the supermarket. For things like rice and flour, there's just not that much room for difference in quality.

- Go to Sunday or farmers' markets. The outing can double as a fun family activity and the produce is usually cheaper and fresher. Pick up something for brunch and you've killed a few birds with one stone.

- Here's a trick to remember in supermarkets: the most expensive items will always be placed at eye height. Look up or down and you'll find, sometimes almost hidden away, a cheaper brand.

- Only eat at restaurants when the food is something you can't easily prepare yourself – e.g. sushi or complicated exotic dishes.

- Make eating out really worth it by choosing places with all you can eat specials. This way you can have breakfast, skip lunch and pig out for dinner. Also keep an eye out for places that have discounts for meals for your children.

- Buy fruit and vegetables in season.

- If you have the space, grow your own spinach, tomatoes and herbs – they cost next to nothing and are a fun way to add nutrients to your meals without spending much.

- Make stock/broth at home. By using bones, vegetable scraps and herbs, you can make an extremely nutritious and tasty base for almost every meal, using things you would have thrown away anyway.

- In the same vein, start a compost heap. Recycling is one of the truest forms of thrift, and your garden will thank you.

- Buy food that doesn't spoil in bulk.

- Buy a healthy snack while you're shopping so that you're not tempted by the rows of chocolates at the checkout line.

- Buy whole fruit and vegetables in minimal packaging.

- Make stews and soups from cheaper cuts of meat.

- Skip organic foods unless it's a really high priority for you. Some vegetables and fruits, like pineapples, are immune to most pests and so don't suffer from exposure to pesticides. Others, especially those that have thin skins or stay on the plant for a long time, benefit more from being organic. Apples, strawberries and bell peppers are notorious for having high pesticide residue, so buy these organic if you can or otherwise scrub them well and eat only occasionally.

- Eat out less frequently but make it more of an event when you do – sometimes a big three course meal in a beautiful restaurant is worth way more than three or four visits to a noisy coffee shop for a quick bite.

- Cook in big batches and put the rest away for later. Otherwise, try roping in friends or family to pool bulk purchases and divide out big quantities of food.

- Try making your own bread. The ingredients are cheap and you might enjoy the process. Plus, fresh, hot homemade bread is pretty hard to beat.

- Eat mindfully and become aware of what triggers you to eat more than you really should. Consider intermittent fasting - seriously. Skipping a meal here and there does wonders for body and mind and saves you the money and energy it takes to prepare food all the time.

- When friends come over, stick to simple meals and ask everyone to pitch in for a potluck style gathering.

- If you see a "2 for 1" deal, check whether you can get the discounted price even if you only buy one.

- At restaurants, avoid padding your bill with overpriced drinks and desserts, most of which are fairly underwhelming. Ask for a glass of water instead and get a filling main dish.

- Pay close attention to food that gets thrown away. Up the quality of your storage to make sure fruits and vegetables aren't spoiling, or buy fresh food in smaller quantities.

- Consider signing up for an online grocery shopping service. You can get your weekly or monthly staples delivered to your door and save both time and effort.

- Take leftover dinner to work or get into the habit of packing a sandwich and a fruit. You'll save hundreds of dollars over the course of a year.

- Think about having a meatless night during the week if you eat meat. A light meal based around eggs or legumes and vegetables is cheap and gives your system a rest.

Clothes

Following food, people can often sacrifice enormous quantities of money on buying clothing. When you're up against a clothing industry that wants to convince you to ditch your entire wardrobe every season and stock it again, this is no mean feat. Clothes can be a touchy area because for so many people, clothes have come to represent self esteem, success, comfort, and a certain image they want to project. Their very identity is bound up with the clothing they wear – a far cry from thinking of clothes as merely protection from the elements.

From a minimalist perspective, if someone truly derives immense pleasure from the creativity and spirit in dressing elaborately and paying for it, the goal is not to suggest that they stop. The minimalist philosophy, as we know by now, is about making sure that only those things that truly serve our highest good are focused on; everything else can be downplayed.

Signs your clothes spending habits are hindering rather than helping: you feel like you are always thinking about what to wear, and never feel satisfied in what you choose; you have tons of clothing and hate all of it; people get frustrated with you because they end up having to take care of buying clothes *for* you; you throw things away before they get worn out; you make impulse purchases; you buy clothing to feel better about yourself – and it doesn't really work... you get the picture.

When you don't have time to spend on clothing

Many men have this attitude to clothing, but deal with their unwillingness to engage with it by fobbing off the responsibility onto wives or mothers. If this works for you, consider yourself spoiled, but otherwise, those who want to look presentable but couldn't be bothered to spend hours in shopping malls have a few other options. If you can, consider hiring a personal shopper to go out and find exactly what you need. Base your new purchases on what has worked in the past, and defer to a stylish friend or work colleagues to give you ideas on what you should go for. Buy quality with the understanding that the better the craftsmanship, the longer you can go without thinking about this problem again.

When you don't have money to spend on clothing

Some of the most painfully chic and creative people have come from backgrounds of poverty. Today, the Internet is teeming with blogs showing you how to turn old or second hand clothing into beautiful pieces that tick all the fashion boxes. If you have the time, learn to sew a little, and nurture the crafter in you to renovate and rework what you already have. When buying new, get wardrobe staples to go with everything in all weather, and make sure the quality of the garment will carry you through a few years.

When you don't have time OR money to spend on clothing

If you don't care at all about clothing and also have no money to spend on it, then, enjoy it! Maybe you're an eccentric college professor, mom of eight or chronic scruffy person. Turn your attention to other areas of your life that do matter.

Action Steps for saving money on clothing expenditure:

- Build a "capsule wardrobe" - high quality pieces in neutral colors that can be combined with almost anything. A multipurpose dress, good trousers, a simple cardigan and a few tops that can all be worn with each other is an excellent wardrobe backbone.

- Avoid sales. If you wouldn't have bought it otherwise, don't buy it now just because it's cheaper.

- Throw out, sell or give away clothing that you plan to wear when you are thinner, more daring etc. A good rule: if it hasn't been worn in a year, it's just taking up space and needs to go.

- Watch out for "dry clean only" garments – dry cleaning costs can really add up.

- Invest in a quality sewing kit to repair torn or damaged clothing. Don't throw broken shoes away: you can often get them fixed or re-soled at dry cleaners for a reasonable fee. Similarly, don't throw away clothing that has become stained. Cover up the stain with dark blue or black dye and the item is as good as new.

- Store clothing properly. When in use, let clothes hang in a well-aired cupboard on padded hangers. If put away for the season, seal in vacuum packed bags or fold away with moth balls to prevent damage.

- Forget about the tumble dryer. Unless it's an emergency and it's rainy, hang your clothes to dry. This saves money and lengthens the life of the material.

- Wash clothing only when it's actually dirty. Especially for top clothing layers that don't touch the skin, a simple airing in a closet will be enough to keep it going for two or three wears. You save on detergent and wear and tear on your clothes.

- Consider switching to natural detergents that are gentler on your clothes, or else try "soap nuts." These are a fun and dirt-cheap alternative - they literally grow on trees and produce natural soap that cleans your clothes when put into the washing machine. You can use them many times over and compost them when you're done (look at wellnessmama.com, an online stockist).

- Iron on the coolest setting to avoid wearing away the fibers.

- Wash lingerie and hosiery by hand using a little hair shampoo, and dry flat.

- For big events like weddings or graduations, buy something simple and elegant enough to be formal, but that can be dressed down and worn again later. A simple black cotton dress in the right cut can become very formal if paired with the right accessories. Think a big statement necklace or luxurious silk scarf. For things like tuxedos or wedding dresses, it's almost always better to rent.

- If you're crafty, use old clothes to make quilts or recycle into other items. At the very least, you can often turn an old garment into cleaning rags or stuffing for a throw pillow.

- Choose clothing in natural fibers. Pure cotton or wool wears well and often won't stretch or fade over time. Leather items can last a lifetime.

Health

Sadly, it usually takes an iffy test result from the doctor or a few days in bed with a serious health issue to remind us how important good health is. Like oxygen, you only notice how much you need it when all of a sudden you don't have it anymore. From a consumerist perspective, good health is often packaged and sold as something purely aspirational. Tapping into our very real fears of death, unattractiveness or both, many people think health is merely another thing to put on the "to do" list. Get the number on the scale right, end of story. How often have you decided to start a new health regime and discovered that your very next step was to *buy* something – a gym membership, running shoes or new vitamins? As with the other areas covered so far, a minimalist approach to budgeting for our health should focus on the core and trim away the time and money-draining extras.

When you don't have time to spend on good health

You *want* to exercise more, sure, but just look at your schedule! This is a little paradoxical, when you think about it. Being in better health means you live longer, in a general sense. You buy yourself more time. Are you sure you want to struggle away at a life that is so demanding it doesn't even allow you to care for your own body? Nevertheless, if time is an issue, decide beforehand, realistically, how much time you can "sacrifice" each week to maintaining your health. Your goal in this case would be to identify the least amount of effort you can put in for the most health benefit. We don't all have to be gym bunnies who eat right. If a run once a week or the occasional dance class is keeping illness at bay, then do that and return your attention to whatever else you find more worthy at that moment.

When you don't have money to spend on good health

A more common but easier to fix problem. Once you stop buying into the idea that you need gadgets and goodies to be healthful, you're halfway there. Don't try bolstering a weak will or lack of interest with dieting apps, special equipment, classes, juicers, books, supplements or outfits. Companies selling these items will advertise hard that they are a key to, even a replacement for, simply doing the work. But don't believe it. The tips that follow will give you some ideas of how to love your body a little without spending much.

When you don't have time OR money to spend on good health

This book has tried to show that once you identify your true passions and values, the work of a budget is to make sure your behavior is aligning with them. The case of not being willing or able to invest anything towards your health is perhaps an exception. You can go a long way abusing your body before it gives out, but health is pretty close to being a non negotiable. If you have no time, money or energy to devote to staying alive and happy, it may be time to start reassessing your priorities.

Action Steps for saving money on health:

- Make friends with Youtube. There you can find workout videos of every kind, from yoga to weight lifting to cardio.

They're free, you have a lot of variety and you can do them at home in your pajamas.

- Healthy eating, with the exception of good quality meat, is usually also cheap. Fill up half your plate with vegetables and you kill two birds with one stone. Leafy greens, eggs, cabbage and tomatoes are healthful and cost very little for the nutrients they provide.

- Really research your vitamins thoroughly and make sure you aren't throwing away money on useless supplements. Homeopathic remedies and special "superfoods" like goji berries have all been shown to have little effect. Save your money. An Omega 3 oil and a general multivitamin are usually more than enough.

- If you go to gym less than 3 or 4 times a week, it's time to get over the fact that it may not be worth it. You'll spend less on drop-in classes that you actually go to.

- Floss!

- If you choose to keep going to gym, make full use of all the amenities there. Shower, use the pool and sauna and take the opportunity to learn about gym equipment you may have avoided. You might even find a handy childcare solution as many gyms have a crèche or children's swimming classes, for instance.

- Don't buy Vitamin C to "boost your immune system". Vitamin C has been shown time and time again to offer no protection against colds and flus.

- Take up walking or running. If you're a beginner you needn't splash out on expensive trainers. A cheaper pair of light trail running shoes will see you through most situations, if you feel you must kit yourself out. Running or walking can double up as a social or meditative activity.

- If you live in a country where you need to buy health insurance, comb over your policy and see if you might downgrade to a smaller plan. Healthy bodies under forty seldom need a full, comprehensive medical plan, as unpopular as that opinion may be .

- Consider getting glasses instead of contact lenses. They may be more convenient, but the cost over years and years will add up. Not to mention that contact lenses pose risks to the health of your eye that glasses don't.

- Depending heavily on where you live, things like hormonal contraception or condoms are often available for free from planned parenthood or community clinics. This saves a nice sum over the course of a year, and you can often get enough for a few months at a time.

- This may sounds silly, but: wash your hands. This is a really simple way to reduce your exposure to viruses and bacteria and consequently, colds and flu.

- It's the unglamorous truth, but sometimes the best health decisions you make are not active decisions at all. Merely refrain from damaging your health deliberately and the battle is half won. Unless it adds immeasurable happiness to your life, quit drinking, smoking or recreational drug use.

- If you insist on smoking, consider rolling your own. It's cheaper and has a certain charm to it.

- Always, always ask if there's a generic medication available.

- Sleep properly and give your body the best defense against stress and disease. Decide on your personal bare minimum and stick to it.

- Drinking water is likewise cheap or free and can only add to your quality of life.

- Vegetable juices are a good way to get your vitamins and can even be cheaper and more convenient than preparing vegetables from scratch.

- Buy cheap disposable razors and sharpen them when they get dull.

- Don't bother with foods labeled as "diet". Speciality cereals, drinks and the like almost always have more affordable alternatives. Ordinary oats are dirt cheap and better for you than cereal, for example.

- Switch to tea instead of coffee and bring your own thermos to work. Tea is a fraction of the cost of coffee, it's healthier and it comes in more fun varieties.

- Build in daily activities that encourage more exercise indirectly. Walk the dog, play with children, dance, build something, etc. Exercise at the gym doesn't hold a candle to exercise that is fun and actually enriches your life.

Home and Cleaning

Is your home a peaceful sanctuary that you return to at the end of a busy day to recharge? Or is it a "gilded cage" that constantly demands your attention to maintain it? The best budget solutions for your household are those that save you time and money, and add to your quality of life, either by removing an annoyance or directly making life more pleasant.

Save time:

- Invest in appliances for chores you need to do everyday, for example a washing machine, dishwasher or pressure cooker. Give away or sell appliances that you use less than once a week. You could likely put their cash value to better use.

- If you can afford to, consider housekeeping help. This may take the form of dropping clothes off at a laundry service or getting a monthly garden service.

- Arrange for debit orders for recurrent payments.

- Shop online and get your regular groceries delivered to you home.

Save money:

- Split costs by carpooling.

- Buy food in bulk from wholesalers and divide between friends and family.

- Unbranded detergent is usually pretty effective but cheaper. Better still are natural cleaners like white vinegar, bleach and bicarbonate of soda.

- Make sure your home is weather proof and seal door and window cracks to save on heating.

- Commit to only having indigenous and low water plants in your garden.

- Unless you are a true collector, don't buy magazines or newspapers. Everything in them is readily available online.

- When you're trying to decide whether to buy something new, give yourself a mandatory "cooling off" period. For smaller purchases, this could be a week, and for larger, up to a month. If you still want it after this time, then go ahead.

- Buy books on a Kindle or get them from the library.

- Try to combine separate car trips to ensure you don't drive around unnecessarily.

- Turn off the TV. You'd be surprised how much junk you're convinced to buy by watching ads, and you'll save electricity and, more importantly, time.

- Only buy prepackaged foods if the time you gain from not chopping and peeling is worth more than their cost.

- It might be worth it to turn your water heater on and off as needed.

- Replace old showerheads with low flow or more efficient shower heads.

- Put a brick in your toilet cistern to displace some water. You'll waste less with each flush.

- Turn lights off when nobody is in the room. Use candles for a cozy atmosphere.

- Buy energy saving bulbs.

- Buy furniture from second hand shops or online. An hour or so of good hunting could save you half the cost of an item in the end.

- The world is becoming more and more digital. Carefully evaluate if you need your full satellite TV package, or get movies and series online instead.

- Have a clothes swap evening with friends to trade clothing you've fallen out of love with.

- A yard sale can be a fun way to connect with neighbors, get rid of junk and make a little profit in the process.

- If you're a crafty type, you might like the sense of satisfaction you feel from learning a new DIY skill. You can save a lot of money by repairing things or making small items yourself.

- Ask a butcher for off cuts or scraps that your dog or cat could enjoy. Quality pet food without fillers generally satisfies your cat or dog in much smaller helpings, too.

- Reuse items you already have. This takes some imagination but is more environmentally sound, cheaper and simpler. Wash and keep jars and bottles to hold spices, or take the time to repair broken items rather than buying new ones.

- Think about what loyalty programs you might benefit from being a part of. Points for shopping at particular stores, discounts on air travel or medical insurance or reduced banking fees all add up and don't require you to scrimp since they are things you already buy.

Children

There's no easy way to say it, but for some, their children can be a real blind spot when it comes to their finances. The sentiment of "nothing but the best" and being able to provide that for their children is strong. And it wouldn't be overstating the case to say that making their children happy and successful is basically the point of many people's lives. Unfortunately, advertising has burrowed its way into many well meaning parents' brains (and pockets!) and convinced them that unless they shower their offspring with material things, they simply aren't being raised right.

As with other things, it can be sobering to settle on what it truly is you want to leave your children with in this life. Material possessions are one thing, but what often mean the most to children are the lessons they learn from their parents. Were their parents fulfilled, dignified people? Did they show them by example how to navigate life? Did they give them skills or a strong sense of self worth or a lifetime of memories that they'll cherish forever?

Budgeting as a parent often feels awful because of the guilt associated with not providing enough for your children. An easy way around this is to consistently train yourself to reorient to basic principles. The really fundamental ones seldom involve material possessions. Ask yourself what each item represents to your children. For example, you may want to send your child to an expensive art camp that tries to encourage children to make friends and be more creative over the summer holidays. Before feeling bad about not being able to afford it, ask yourself what the value of it truly is. If you hope to teach your child the value in creativity and out of the box thinking, what better way can you show them this lesson than by being creative yourself? Embark on an art project together, build or grow something as a family. You save money and in the process deepen your connection to your child.

Action Steps for saving money on parenting:

- For younger children, practice "toy cycling". Let your child play with one or two main toys and put the rest away. Children can't focus on too many things at once anyway, and when they tire of their current toys, switch them out and it'll be as if they were new. Have a few cycles of toys and you'll encourage more focus and appreciation for each one.

- Choose toys that encourage creative thinking, building or imagination. Cards, balls and simple art supplies give you endless possibilities.

- Give parenting books a skip. At best you'll get a few obvious tips on how not to kill your children accidentally, and at worst they'll turn you into a paranoid parent who needs to buy more parenting books.

- Similarly, Baby Einstein style products are largely a scam. You don't need to spend money on making sure that your child is mentally stimulated. Have you ever really seen a two year old? The world is their playground. Everything is new and wild to them. Have faith that their brains are not going to wither unless you buy them a fancy new baby development program when they're only two months old.

- Give children aged from five up household responsibilities and chores. This builds their sense of competence, keeps them occupied and takes a little off your plate. For instance, delegate feeding the pets to your 6 year old, and they'll learn responsibility as well as give you one less thing to worry about.

- Focus children's birthday parties around fun activities and avoid spending it on table decorations or expensive cake. Children love being the center of attention on their birthdays, and this can be achieved with games and rituals, rather than splashing out on expensive party trinkets.

- Children's hair can usually be cut at home.

- Up to a certain age, children don't care about the kind of clothing they wear or what their room looks like. A 2 year old cannot appreciate the adorable baby booties you spent a fortune on and will be outgrown in a few months, but they certainly will benefit from a college fund that their parents had the foresight to begin early on.

- Leave children at home when you go shopping if possible. You'll need an iron will to turn down a nagging child pushing you to buy that toy or treat.

- Instead of just giving children an allowance and leaving it at that, try to teach them age-appropriate saving and investing skills early on. Have them open a savings account so they can learn how interest works. Help them make goals for big purchases they want and encourage them to be enterprising and spin up money through mowing lawns, selling baked goods or starting a paper route.

- Don't give children too many options. Child psychologists have shown that too much variety can be stressful for younger minds. Tone it down and you'll likely be surprised by how children naturally gravitate towards simplicity when given the chance.

Debt and Finances

Psychologically, debt is a horrible place to be in. The smart use of credit is a skill every financially savvy adult needs to master, but at the same time, less debt is almost always better. There are the obvious golden rules when it comes to credit, namely only incur credit for very large purchases or those that appreciate over time, and always pay down the most expensive debt first, which is usually your credit card.

Consider yourself lucky if you are budgeting to save more or merely downsize your lifestyle - paying down credit is another ball game and requires even more dedication. Fortunately there are resources out there to help people get on top of their debt. If you find your debt is spinning out of control, it's urgent that you get professional help as soon as possible. Remedying a full-blown debt crisis is beyond the scope of this book, although the tips and ideas outlined here will still be of use.

A financial advisor or coach can give you sound advice for a plan to tackle debt and manage finances better. Here are some tips to take control:

- Try to save each month, no matter what. Even if you can only manage a small amount, save it. Saving puts you in a special frame of mind. You are telling yourself that no matter how small your goals are, they are worth pursuing diligently.

- Push yourself to overpay on your mortgage or credit card repayments. A few extra hundred now could mean years saved down the line.

- Consider selling your car. You can save on the cost of a car by buying from auctions, second hand dealers or even rental companies who sell second hand rental models. New cars should be bought with their cost-to-maintain as the primary focus.

- Re-evaluate your insurance payments each month. There are almost always hidden fees and extras that you didn't notice before.

- Service your car regularly. You won't notice a car that is running less than efficiently, but you will notice the money you save on fuel when you keep your car well maintained.

- If you're flying, book flights as early as humanly possible. Try Skyscanner online to compare rates across airlines, and you could save a lot without even trying.

- Look in to the world of housesitting for when you are away on vacation, or else as an alternative to paying for hotel accommodation. Housesitting is where you agree to watch and take care of someone's home while they're away in exchange for rent. There are millions of resources and profile sites online to hook up with people who are looking for house sitters. Alternatively try "couchsurfing" which is more informal.

- Look at taking a small course in personal finance management. Local colleges might offer short programs or else find an online course.

- Switch to a bank with lower fees. You may even convince your current bank to cut you a deal.

- Consider installing a water or electricity meter into your home. Depending on where you live, this should be quite easy to do and will save you a ton. Getting constant feedback about how much you are spending on things you take for granted means you'll invariably use them more wisely.

- See if you can change your phone contract to a pay as you go option, then give yourself a monthly limit to stick to. Otherwise, try to shift most of your communication to free or cheap platforms like Skype, email or Whatsapp.

- Whatever you do, stop buying lottery tickets. The lottery has rightly been called "idiot tax" and there is just no logical reason for you to literally throw money away on it. Likewise, curb most or all of your gambling, if you do.

- Arrange for an accountant to look over your tax return and give you some advice on what can be written off as tax exempt. More efficiently filed reports could save you hundreds of dollars with zero change to your lifestyle.

- Also make sure you are claiming any government benefits you are entitled to. This may not be a lot on the face of it, but certain benefits really add up over time.

- This may seem obvious, but make a serious effort to stop speeding. Your efforts scrimping and saving in one area could be undone in the one minute you decided to speed on the highway. If you do get fines, pay them quickly to avoid incurring any penalties.

- If you have a problem with frittering away cash, make it a habit to only carry a small amount of cash on you and use cards instead. The extra effort to use this or draw at an ATM can deter many impulse buys. Plus, you'll be able to see very clearly where everything went on your monthly statement.

- If you have a problem with abusing your credit card, hide it away somewhere at home instead of keeping it on you. You'll be forced to think through any purchase more clearly.

- Speaking of statements, get them emailed to you and you can use any of the thousands of handy apps out there designed to manage the data.

Miscellaneous tips and tricks

- Sign up for a course on Coursera.com. These are top-notch university level courses on everything from business to programming to linguistics, and can be done for free in the privacy of your own home. A lower key option for self improvement without breaking the bank is watching a daily TED talk or downloading some classic novels on Kindle, many of which are in the public domain and free, too.

- Museums, galleries and even zoos are good choices for money-conscious outings.

- Keep a literal piggy bank. It's good to have a visual reminder of your savings, and you can dedicate the result to pay for something special. Get into the habit of cleaning out your wallet or pockets at the end of the day and feeding your piggy.

- Wherever possible, walk, cycle or take public transport. This doubles up as great exercise.

- When driving, keep your speed and acceleration as constant as possible. Avoiding sudden stops or erratic driving saves wear and tear on car parts as well as fuel.

- Become familiar with your library. Most libraries are about so much more than just the books. See what classes, talks or performances they have, and try checking out magazines, DVDs or music.

- Buy Christmas and birthday gifts early on. To avoid the situation where people are gifted piles of unnecessary and sort of unwanted stuff, give gift vouchers instead. If you're worried about this being too impersonal, give a gift card together with a more thoughtful item like handmade cookies. These are cheap to make and always welcome, plus you can make them in a batch to give to everyone over the holiday period. Alternatively try a "secret Santa" format for Christmas with everyone writing down what they'd like. Making Christmas dinner a potluck affair means less stress and financial burden on just one or two people.

- Go drinking during happy hour only.

- Choose easy to maintain hairstyles that don't require constant upkeep. This means ditching relaxers, heat stylers that sap hours of your life and damage your hair, and hair color that needs professional attention every six weeks.

Chapter 6: The Challenge - Putting everything into practice

The trick to minimalist budgeting is finding what works for you, and continually working to zoom in on the lifestyle that is optimized to make you the happiest while spending the least amount of time, money and energy. Too many budgeting gurus will give you ample advice on how to maximize on only one variable, which doesn't succeed because the other variables suffer.

So even though you've sliced through your monthly expenses, your state of mind has become so miserly and anxious that you can't enjoy the money you're supposed to be saving. Or you try so hard to find the sweet spot between your financial resources and your own happiness that you don't notice the hours of your life you throw away to save a crumb here and there. I had this thought when I read a post by a popular homemaker and blogger. Her advice on how to save a few dollars by sewing her own dishcloths was at odds with the time and effort she had clearly squandered in putting together a professional two thousand word tutorial with several photographs taken with a high end camera.

Let's turn our attention to some hypothetical people who decided to approach their budgeting from a minimalist perspective. It doesn't take a genius to understand that to budget well, one must simply find ways to either spend less money or make more. That's it. Any advice over and above that is frankly condescending. The budget guru will ask if you buy gasoline and if so, will tell you to buy less. Wasting a lot of money on fantasy action figures each month? Then stop doing that, the budget guru will tell you.

Minimalist budgeting takes a broader look and asks you to consider what it really means to have "less" or "more", and why you should care. One man's suffering is another man's luxury living, so it pays to get to the bottom of this value judgment first, rather than simply assuming less is always more, and in always the same way. After we look at some hypothetical people's budgets, you may get a more inspired view of how to start constructing your own. Not through tricks and hacks and finding the courage to just say no, but with a conscious, deliberate consideration of what is important.

Case Study 1 – Amanda's uphill battle

Amanda always felt like a tiny hurricane was constantly whirling around her head. Raising three children under ten, she felt deficient in every way possible. She worked herself half to death but found her salary just barely covering costs. She was exhausted to the bone but couldn't take even one day off of her life to get the rest she deserved. Her solution up till then had been to take on more at work to try to pay for a nanny, but there was only so much she could pay. Her husband's job kept them afloat for the most part, but the relationship between them had barely any time to thrive in the flurry of everyday responsibilities. Every day of Amanda's life ended with her in bed at night, quietly wondering to herself whether this was all there was to life.

Amanda sat down with her husband and drew up a comprehensive accounting of where every cent of their money was going, as well as every second of their time. Rather than merely counting up money in versus money out, they also looked at what value they were deriving from their children, their home, their jobs. What emerged was how little pleasure any of it gave Amanda. Everything was a chore. There was no time or money to do what she wanted. Her reward for managing to juggle all the balls she had to was merely to do it all over again the next day.

Things needed to change. Amanda discovered that a lot of stress arose from housework for their frankly large house. They decided that within 6 months, they wanted to move to a house that was smaller and easier to care for. They found new homes for their demanding pets. Amanda took a long hard look at her life and realized how little of it served her. It was a tough decision to make, but she realized that owning a home with the stereotypical white picket fence, husband, kids and two dogs was not really, when she looked closely, what she wanted for herself.

Her next step was to negotiate a part time schedule with her work. She agreed to work remotely at home for a few hours each day for greatly reduced pay. Rather than crash the family financially, Amanda found renewed vigor and decided that she would like to homeschool her children. What emerged is that when she had a close, loving and involved relationship with them, the pressing need to escape on vacation lessened. Becoming more involved with her children gave her a renewed sense of purpose, and the family saved money on schooling, after school care and babysitters.

As they transitioned, there were moments when Amanda had to get used to their new, downsized lifestyle, but when she considered the time and happiness she gained in exchange it seemed worth it. After a few months she realized how little the trappings of middle class life actually meant to her anyway. With free time to spend watching her children grow, the opportunity to connect again with her husband and the relief from not having to run like a rat in a wheel, the changes she had to make in her expenditure felt pretty manageable.

A few years down the line, Amanda followed her dreams a little further and found that "homesteading" was immensely fulfilling. She took courses on how to build her own house and how to farm her own food at home. She raised goats and chickens and even started to coach other people on how to live a more natural, self-sufficient lifestyle.

None of this would have happened if Amanda had merely learnt to deal with her crummy life a little bit better, i.e. made a budget to cut her expenses. Amanda's problem was not that she needed tips and tricks to squeeze in more work hours or stretch a dollar even more to care for her family, it was that she had lost her center of value. In finding her principles, the need to budget became redundant over time.

Case Study 2 – Kim's 3 in 1 solution

Kim had never been a spendthrift. As a matter of fact, she was raised to be frugal and money conscious, and had always kept track of her money habits well enough. When she evaluated her lifestyle in detail, though, one thing was clear: she had a problem with buying clothing. Whereas every other area of her life was under control, including food, entertainment and how much she spent on her home, she had a nasty habit of buying clothes she didn't need and seldom wore anyway. She hated her job and felt it was a way to ease stress, pass the time and inject a little beauty and excitement into her life. But when she looked at how much more she spent on clothes than she did on buying books or exercising making friends or hobbies or trying new things, she had to admit that the ratio was very off.

Kim had tried unsuccessfully to just stop before. After thinking it over very carefully, she realized that shopping clothes *was* her hobby. In a job that stifled her creativity, she found that buying beautiful clothes was the only outlet for her to indulge in creative expression. No wonder she was unwilling to give it up! Kim decided not to cut down, but to re-channel her resources to where it really mattered.

After tallying up the cost she usually spent on clothing each month, she vowed to take that money and buy a sewing machine instead. She made a new hobby of going to thrift stores and finding cheap items that she then revamped into amazing creations that she got immense joy and pride out of. She also joined a knitting group and made friends there with other similarly minded people. They encouraged her to get more joy out of her creative urges.

At the end of the day, the total money spent is more or less the same for Kim. But what she gained in quality of life means she was using her resources smartly. By rerouting the money she spent on a pointless shopping habit, she cut down on unnecessary spending, made new friends and found a hobby that not only saved her money, it enriched her life. It may even be that in five years' time, Kim has discovered that her passion for creative clothing is lucrative. She might open her own boutique or write a How To book sharing her knowledge. What started as a way to save money could well turn into a way to *make* money.

Case Study 3 – Jeff's Dilemma

Like a lot of people his age, Jeff had been trying to break away from under his parents' wings and get his life started. He had a few problems. While looking for work, he couldn't realistically afford the rent to get his own apartment, but he was slowly going crazy staying with his folks. While he was constantly short on cash, he had lots of free time. His self esteem took a beating the longer he stayed home and had his parents pay for him. What's worse, he was getting depressed and out of shape.

Jeff's challenge was to transform the excess time he had into money and quality of life. He sat down and organized his priorities. He needed to keep his spirits up, find a job and get out of the house as quickly as possible. He decided he would volunteer for a few days a week at a community center and offer to help coach a children's football team. The position paid nothing, but Jeff made connections, kept motivated and spent large amounts of time away from his parents. He also connected with someone who offered to help him put together a CV. He conveniently had access to regular, free exercise which got him feeling better about life in general, and discovered that the satisfaction he got from bonding with the children gave him the motivation to find work.

Chapter 7: A Note on "Poverty"

People can be strange about money. Something about our culture ties self worth so strongly into the number value of how much we earn and own, that your social class becomes as much a part of you as your hair color or occupation.

A lot of budget/thrift resources out there will skim around this topic or pretend it's not even there. Wanting to cut down on expenses because you care about the environment? Great. All power to you. Want to get rid of some of your stuff because you crave "simplicity" in your life? Excellent, how very enlightened of you. Scratching around for coupons because, well, you're poor? Hm, not so good.

The principles of minimalism followed here in this book don't assume any level of wealth in particular. Minimalism is about getting down to essentials, and the essentials are different for each person. What's important is the *spirit* behind the material things and the money. It's possible for a very wealthy person to live a minimalist lifestyle, and it's possible for someone living on the poverty line to be living a materialistic one. What is "enough" or "simple" for one is extravagant for another.

That being said, many people come to minimalism at least in part out of necessity. For some, being laid off at work or trying to absorb the cost of a new child or other blow to their finances forces them to reconsider their lifestyle. What begins as a failure to keep up within the capitalist system as we understand it turns out to be an opportunity to step outside of that system and look at it for what it is.

It's not nice to say, but very often the feeling is that voluntary frugality is somehow nobler than the involuntary kind. Living off of government handouts and scraping by on cheap food and rent just doesn't have the same shine to it as a pretty stay at home mom who sews her children's clothing in her free time because her husband's salary gives her the luxury to.

It's important to recognize that the choice to live minimally, the ability to identify your priorities and work with them, is a privilege, and it's own kind of wealth. Those stuck in cyclic, long-term poverty are often so tired and cynical that it's almost a luxury to take the time to meditate on their values, hopes and dreams. So, yes, poverty is not the same as minimalism. But wherever your hard limits come from, minimalism can help with the *spirit* behind finding a way to work with them.

The approach in this book is designed to appeal to everyone, but of course, you may have read something and thought,

"Wow, that is totally not how my life works." and felt a little alienated. I know it's happened a few times that I've heard someone talk about "cutting down" on this or that expense – and their new value is so much higher than my upper limit that it's almost embarrassing. But don't let things like this deter you. The principles remain the same, whether you think $10 is a lot of money or whether you wouldn't even notice if it fell out of your wallet.

Minimalism is about being real. The case studies so far have been short and necessarily a little simplistic. Sometimes, there isn't enough money, enough time *or* enough energy. No matter which way you spin it or what you reshuffle, there just isn't enough to go around. This ties in with how we think about budgeting in general, and that sickening feeling you may feel when you hear that word. Sometimes in life, you have to go without.

What does minimalism have to say about, well, being poor?

The time element, as we've discovered, is nonnegotiable. Money can be earned, but there are also, to varying degrees, limits to what we can earn and how little we can spend. The only area that can be controlled the most by us is the subjective value we assign to money, to things. We can control how we look at our achievements, how we think about money and our own happiness. Learning that we can still be happy and fulfilled and have a life that is as rich as anybody else's, no matter how in debt we may be, is a hard but sweet lesson to learn.

If you find these issues frequently touch a nerve, your path to minimalism may include an exploration of your own attitudes towards and relationship with money. The psychology of money is complicated. If you are in the mindset of an ascetic, or are unconsciously punishing yourself by doing with less, you are no less entwined and obsessed with material possessions as the ostentatious show off you are trying not to be like. There is a reason people give away their possessions after deciding they want to commit suicide. Minimalism is about being mindful of material things and how they interact with your world and your happiness. Though we all come to minimalism with a different background, set of values and goals, the principles are the same for us all.

Chapter 8: A Note on Marriage and Money

Stress around money constitutes the most common reason that marriages fail. Who pays for what and why can be so stressful a concept to negotiate that some couples end up separating before they figure it out. In a marriage partnership, there are two income sources (usually) and more complicated expenditures. Add children and the complexity increases even more still.

But the basic principles of money management hold true. In partnerships, each person's contributions and rights to shared wealth need to be very thoroughly understood. As a couple or a family, you need to regularly do check ups on what everyone is bringing to the table (and, um, taking off of the table...)

Many men unwittingly put themselves into damaging financial binds with their wives, and wives can unwittingly fall into the homemaker role and shoot themselves in the financial foot when it comes to their own personal savings and retirement. As you sit down with your spouse or partner, tally up income that stems from all areas, including the more abstract ones of time and value. Stay at home mothers may contribute nothing in the way of money but single handedly enhance the value of the household through raising children, as well as saving time and energy by taking on the management of the household. A good accounting will recognize all of this in the decision making process. A better accounting will see how well this picture aligns with both of your values and principles.

Chapter 9: The First Steps To Your Own Minimalist Budget

So, are you ready to begin your own minimalist budget story?

Week One

Hopefully, by now, you have a stronger sense of how the principles outlined here will apply to your specific lifestyle. In this first week, your goal will seem like the simplest but will in fact be the most important step. Here, you will find your "core" around which you will structure the rest of your budget. Without this core, your budget goals are meaningless and you're unlikely to stick to them for long.

For the time being, just plan. Keep the three elements – time, money and value – in mind. Look with honest and realistic eyes at the time that is available to you. It may help to draw up a schedule that shows, in hours, where all your time goes. If you're a visual person, block these out in different colors – the effect can really hit home when it's staring you in the face in neon pink and yellow. You may tally up how many hours you spend on various activities, i.e. sleep, work, chores, eating, relaxing etc.

Next, have a very rough idea of your overall income and your overall expenditure for a month period. This doesn't have to be 100% accurate for now, but be in the general ballpark. Don't guess – go on what records you have.

Lastly, and this is the most important part, meditate a little on your goals, values and passions. What adds to your life? What makes you happy and fulfilled? What gives you purpose? When are the moments in your schedule that bring you the most joy? Make a note of them.

Now, be curious about emerging patterns. As mentioned earlier on, you may find it helpful to have a column that ranks each category according to how valuable it is in your life. Do this with percentages or rank them in order. This will let you see if the actual time, money and energy you spend in any one area actually makes sense when you consider how much meaning it brings you.

Start to hone in on some goals for yourself. Choose what looks like the stickiest area – there will always be one! The one with the biggest discrepancy between your subjective appraisal and how much money you spend on it, the item that shocks you, *that's* the one to start with.

Week Two

With a little bit of direction, make a goal to work on for the rest of the month. One goal may not seem like much, but in many cases the biggest problem is usually one specific area that, if addressed, would help everything else fall into place. Remember to make your goals SMART. Specific, measurable, attainable, realistic and time based goals are the only ones you'll be able to achieve, so take some time making a good, solid goal.

Sit down with a calendar and map out the time frame/s for your goals/s. It's a good idea to break down bigger goals into smaller ones and then have them spaced out over a realistic time frame. So, start with the goal of spending 10% less on groceries, and then move onto 20% and more gradually over the course of six months.

Your goals could be money based or have to do with how you allocate the resources you already have. Your goal could also be to simply get more enjoyment out of the money you spend. Once you have some realistic goals laid out, you need to commit to them. If you've chosen them wisely, your goals shouldn't be some Herculean task that takes mountains of will power. In fact, you should feel energized and keen to reach these goals because they are all about getting you closer to the lifestyle you actually value.

The Next Month

Over the course of the month, keep a close eye on your goal. Notice if the goal needs adjusting and don't be afraid to tweak it if it's not quite right. Mindful budgeting means making smart decisions, it isn't about punishing yourself or forcing yourself to do with less when you can't or don't want to. With a firmer idea of what your core principles are, the less important details can be shuffled around without too much stress.

Try to avoid pushing yourself to make too many changes at once as this actually increases the chance you'll revert back to old habits. Go slowly and step by step. Importantly, don't let anyone tell you what you should and shouldn't value. If you really feel like a particular item will add something to your life, get it. If after a while of budgeting and assessing your goals you discover you could completely do away with the things you're supposed to need, just do it.

Six Months and Beyond

As you start ticking off your goals, you may be inspired to make more or to turn to maintaining your lifestyle. Your journey will be your own, but if you regularly take the time to check in with your core values and beliefs, your choices will never be too far removed from those that will ultimately make your life more meaningful.

In the end, budgeting is just a natural extension from a way of looking at life in general. It is pointless to ask yourself to cut down your spending so that you are only buying the "essentials" when you haven't actually defined what is essential for your life. A budget is only as good as the purpose it's meant to fulfill, and only you can decide what that purpose is.

Saving money is easy. Earn more, spend less. That's about it, really. The reason why so many people fail to make something so simple work for them is because money is not, as we've been taught, an objective, static thing. It's bound up in our histories, our psychology and our own personal values. A budget that has any chance of being actually implemented must take into account these values. In fact, these values have to be the main inspiration.

Moving forward:

Life is short. Money and material things can make our time on this earth better, and they can help us inch closer to what we find meaningful and worthwhile. *But, they are not meaningful and worthwhile in themselves.* This short book has been about examining this relationship between money and happiness. The goal of a revamped and better budget is never to just save money, rather, to make your spending and earning habits match more closely with what your life really is and what you really want it to be. Saving money when you feel directionless and living a life without purpose counts for very little.

Additional Resources

Here are a few possibly useful websites and books that you may find interesting on your budget journey:

Mint.com. This is a great site that helps you manage your accounts, create and monitor a budget and track your savings and investments. It takes a little time to learn the ropes but is invaluable once you do.

BudgetPulse.com is a free app that allows you to enter in transactions, income and savings.

Wellnessmama.com sells soapnuts in the USA, but a quick Google search will show you vendors in your country. Get a small trial bag to see if you like them, first. There are also occasionally stores that sell soap nut trees, seemingly just so you can make the joke about washing powder growing on trees.

Honestlywtf.com is a fun style blog that shows you how to put together fashion DIY projects, usually for very cheap. There are about a zillion others though, so if you don't like the look of this one, search "recessionista", fashion DIY or second hand clothing in your area. Instructables.com also has detailed DIY projects, crafts, hacks and recipes for the budding tinkerer in you. Many of them are kid friendly, too.

Thesixitemschallenge.wordpress.com is a great site explaining the philosophy behind trying to live with only six items of clothing. Readers share their journeys of how they choose their special six items, and how they used creativity and simplicity to spin up new outfits each day for 30 days.

Eyeslipsface.com is an online cosmetics company that sells dirt cheap make up that is pretty effective. Some products cost only $1, and fans swear it's a dollar well spent.

Thekrazycouponlady.com, groupon.com and other coupon and discount sites let you lop off up to 75% of the cost of food, vacations, services... basically anything. Sign up for a few and see if you can save on vacations, manicures or restaurant meals.

Allrecipes.com has a handy feature that lets you enter in the ingredients you have and search for a recipe to match. They also offer full menus, shopping lists and dinner party plans, as well as recipes designed for a stricter budget.

Theminimalistmom.com – a great blog about thrifty living with a minimalist spin.

Thefrugalgirl.com has lots of good resources for frugal living and tips that fit in well with a minimalist lifestyle.

Google Mary Potter Kenyan for some fun tips on using coupons to save money.

Craigslist.com may have a shady reputation, but you can often find really good deals on second hand furniture or appliances. Also look at whether someone is giving something away for free or willing to barter.

Tinyhouseblog.com is an eye opener. See how people live in and love their exceptionally tiny houses, taking the minimalist philosophy to some interesting extremes. Also great for DIYers or homesteaders.

Etsy.com is great place to sell homemade goods for a small supplement to your income. People sell textile crafts, food items and art. Also check out freelancer.com, odesk.com or guru.com for freelance gigs that could offset some of your expenses. Constant Content is an online gallery to showcase articles and sell them to interested parties. A good article can sell for $50 - 100.

Budgetsaresexy.com has an enormous library of free, printable budget templates that you can use, whatever your budgeting needs.

Ourfreakingbudget.com is a humorous blog about a couple's journey out of debt and into more money and value conscious living. Lots of useful tips and templates. Great for couples or those with young children.

GasBuddy is an American tool that lets you compare fuel prices in your area so you can go with the lowest one.

Track your Credit score for free with Creditkarma.com. Again, for US users.

Sparkplugging.com is a treasure of resources for those who work from home or want to make a little spare money in their downtime.

Helium.com and HubPages are also options for spinning a little extra passive income by writing articles and getting a share of the ad revenue they receive.

Chrisguillebeau.com is a pretty inspirational blog called The Art of Non-Conformity and will motivate you to keep your unconventional dreams alive.

The book "Smart Women Finish Rich: 9 Steps to Achieving Financial Security and Funding Your Dreams" by David Bach is a great book for women who may have put off sorting their finances out. With more of a savings/investment focus, this book is great if you'd like to become better with money in general. There are plenty of books geared towards women and finance as, sadly, this is not a skill out culture tends to encourage in the fairer sex.

The book "Exterminate Your Debt Forever" by Carol Mills is another great book that will help you get out from under the mountain of debt that's holding you back. Short, but very practical.

The book "Essentialism: The Disciplined Pursuit of Less" by Greg McKeown is another brilliant book about simplicity and the fine art of doing with less. Great if you're interested in some of the principles outlined in this book.

The book "Canning for a New Generation: Bold, Fresh Flavors for the Modern Pantry" by Liana Krissoff is another great book. Preserving food is a fun hobby and economical as well.

The book "Zen Mind, Beginner's Mind" by Shunryu Suzuki is one of the quintessential books on Zen Buddhism; in it you may find some happy parallels with minimalism.

Conclusion

Money is a resource, and a very important one, but it is not the only metric of success or efficiency. You can change your life entirely without saving a cent by learning to think of what you have differently. Conventional budgeting offers a narrow view, a purely mechanistic perspective on money. Want more of it? Spend less of it. Invest. Save.

But money is a tool and how we spend it is an expression of our values and what we think is important. How much would you pay for peace of mind and the calm you get from knowing you are living well? How much of your life do you give away when you work? How much of that do you recoup in the form of your salary? Of all your expenses, have you remembered to include the time you waste stressing about money?

These may seem like vague or overly philosophical questions, but they get to the root of how we earn, spend and think of money. Once we understand these roots, our efforts to save here and there not only become easier, they become more meaningful.

Finally, I would love to hear how this book has helped you, so if you liked this book I would really appreciate it if you'd leave a review and tell me all about it. You can leave a review by searching for the title of this book on www.amazon.com.

Bonus: Preview of "Minimalism: How To Declutter, De-Stress and Simplify Your Life With Simple Living"

Today, a growing number of people are becoming dissatisfied with their lives and turning to simpler ways of working, living and raising their children. This book will explore the philosophy of minimalism and how it can streamline your life, declutter your home, reduce stress and reconnect you to what's truly important.

You'll find ways to adopt a mindset that promotes simplicity and elegance in your every day life, and rethink your dependence on material possessions. Whether in our wardrobes, kitchens, work lives or our deeper sense of personal and spiritual purpose, we could all do with focusing on things that align with our values and reducing the distraction of those things that pull us away from them. This book shows you how.

For those born and raised in the height of our consumer society, the idea that happiness and personal fulfillment is found in *stuff* is more or less a given. The capitalist machine we all live within requires only one thing of us: that we should constantly want, and the things we should want are to be found, usually, in malls. Malls that are filled with strategically placed advertising, with the sole purpose to entice and lure you, trying to convince you that you need, not want, their specific product. Our economy relies heavily on a steady stream of consumption: better clothes, cars, bigger houses and things to fill those houses with, the newest appliances, Christmas decorations, pet toys, jewelry, office furniture, pot plants, gaming consoles, specialty tires, luxury soaps... the array of stuff is simply dazzling.

But if you are reading this there's a chance you find this overabundance just a little... exhausting. Paradoxically, there seems to be a sad sort of emptiness in filling up one's life with more things. What is simple and truly valuable often seems to be completely hidden under mountains of what is unnecessary. Although advertising tells us the best way to solve problems is to *buy* solutions, tranquility and a graceful life seem to elude us, no matter what we buy or how much of it.

Minimalism is an aesthetic, a philosophy and a way of life. This book takes a look at how deeply liberating a simpler life can be, and shows you ways you can adopt a calmer, more deliberate way of living and working. Minimalism is about clearing away the clutter that is distracting from what is really important. It's about rethinking our attitudes to ownership, to our lifestyles and to our innermost values.

This book will give practical advice on owning fewer clothes, de-cluttering your life, simplifying your daily routine and reducing mindless consumerism. It will also explore how practical changes to our surroundings can lead to a previously unknown inner peace and calm.

Other Books By This Author

- Minimalism: How To Declutter, De-Stress And Simplify Your Life With Simple Living

- How To Stop Worrying and Start Living – What Other People Think Of Me Is None Of My Business: Learn Stress Management and How To Overcome Relationship Jealousy, Social Anxiety and Stop Being Insecure

- Mindful Eating: A Healthy, Balanced and Compassionate Way To Stop Overeating, How To Lose Weight and Get a Real Taste of Life by Eating Mindfully

- Self-Esteem For Kids - Every Parent's Greatest Gift: How To Raise Kids To Have Confidence In Themselves And Their Own Abilities

23196328R00055

Made in the USA
Middletown, DE
19 August 2015